Matt I̶t̶a̶m̶...

A Love Story

By

Dan Kreuter

Matthew Adam Kreuter
November 3, 1989 · May 17, 2022

MATT MAN: A LOVE STORY

Ordering Information: Quantity sales. Special discounts are available on quantity purchases by corporations, associations, and others. Orders by U.S. trade bookstores and wholesalers.

DREAMSTARTERS

www.DreamStartersPublishing.com

Table of Contents

My Addict – A Love Story.. 6
EARLY DAYS 11
Tuesday 12
Philadelphia Love Song 14
Big Mike 16
A Walk in the Sun.. 20
Blues and Despair 23
No Blues.. 24
Jesus Christ 25
Long Live the Blues 26
Confetti 27
How Long? 28
Getting to the top 29
Like Eating Glass.. 30
Toxicity 31
Psychodrama Poppy Flower.. 32
Stars and Symbols 33
Love Poems.. 34
Scranton Girl 35
Kind of Girl.. 37
Sunken Stone... 38
Trying to Recover 39
My Pen and I.. 40
Recovery... 41
Lightning Storm Lightning Storm Redux.................................... 42
Lightning 43
Lightning Storm 44
Lightning Storm Redux.. 45
LAST DAYS... 46
Heart Cooks Brain 47
The Awakening 48
Be There Soon... 49
Halcyon Bells.. 50
IOUs... 51
Water... 52
Water & Fire 53

MATT MAN: A LOVE STORY

Acknowledgements to Karen, Mike and Breanne:

We made it through the darkness together, which allows us to truly love the light

To Matt's friends and relatives:

Please remember his spirit and his love for life

To those of you who manufacture, enable, and distribute Fentanyl:

You know who you are.
I don't blame you, but I'll never forgive you.

Me and my boy

My Addict – A Love Story

This is not a cautionary tale, nor a prescription to success when dealing with an addict.

My addict was my flesh & blood – he was our son. "Was" because he died on May 17, 2022 from a Fentanyl overdose. Age 32. I still have his sixty-day sober coin. He died less than sixty days later.

If addiction is truly a disease, as it is said, his disease was of the incurable variety. He took me & my wife and our other son to some dark and ugly places. But I loved him, and still love him. He disgraced our family. But I loved him and still love him. He lied to us and deceived us, but I loved him and still love him. He caused us great stress and anxiety and put our lives in peril. But I loved him and still love him.

As the parents of an addict, we cared so deeply– we did everything right and we did everything wrong.

We know that the victim of the serial killer is not to blame for the shooter's wonton, unthinkable actions– and yet there is always the aftermath of what would have been, what should have been, what could have been, if only…

We all love our children, and we often overrate them, because love is blind.

But Matt was a talented boy, a natural in everything he did. He was a "mannish boy;" alert, active and so capable at such a young age, he was nicknamed "Matt Man." High-energy, charismatic, charming, funny and sweet. Like so many others he got caught up in "Oxies" and graduated from there. It's incomprehensible why a healthy, radiant boy who embraced life and was cherished and beloved, would become a tragic and destructive addict!

Early on, he played many sports well and ultimately fell in love with golf, played on his High School team and was close to a scratch handicap. But in the last year of his life, he didn't touch a golf club. Another kind of scoring was far more important.

Along with a love of sports, Matt was a natural mimic, well-read, and a foodie who loved to travel and was deeply into music. He wrote beautifully and somehow, miraculously, in the later helter-skelter years before he died, we rescued some of his writings and poems which are shared here. If you have interest in reading them, I hope you enjoy them. Should you have a loved one in the grip of addiction, perhaps they will find some inspiration or at least something relatable here.

Drug addiction steals your soul and hijacks your mind and ultimately your body. As noted earlier, I have no real answers. The only real motivation in life, in general and in fighting addiction, is self-motivation.

Perhaps the most significant thoughts I can share are:

- Intervene early
- Intervene hard
- Don't worry about your loved one's school, job, and career. This is life and death.

It's sad to say, but like certain terminal diseases, there exists terminal addiction. I think the higher the IQ, the harder it is to unravel.

Along with the "selfish" (in the good sense) emotions and pain we are feeling, there is a constant dull, aching feeling of observing a life wasted, which makes it unbearably sad and so hard to fathom.

There is certainly a sense of shame that comes with the sadness. Where did we go wrong? Where did he go wrong? We shun homeless addicts on the street and shield our eyes, yet we had one in our family. How did this happen? Why did it happen to us? As a family we were so happy and together...pre-addiction. What did we do to have our happiness and optimism snatched from us and replaced with fear and dread? Life isn't fair, I get it, but nobody expects this or plans for it.

A full-fledged addict has three clear-cut paths:

- Rehab & abstinence
- Jail
- Death

Please, please don't pity me. This slim book is my therapy and a gift to the world from a beautiful individual who couldn't turn the corner, and who left this earth after only 32 years. To those of you who lose teenagers and 20-somethings who were murdered- yes, murdered- by Fentanyl laced pills, I can only imagine the pain and emotional torture you felt and will always feel. We are together in a horrid club; those of us who have lost our son, our daughter, our brother, our sister, husband, wife - far, far too soon, for reasons that make no sense.

- Our club has no entry-fee but it comes with a lifetime membership.
- Our club straddles all socio-economic classes.
- Our club picks its members because no one would willingly join it.

To my fellow club members: life goes on, we must look to the future, and we must love and help our children and grandchildren as best we can. We must honor and cherish the pre-addict person we have lost for their good soul that was snatched from us before their life was extinguished.

Maybe, just maybe, we can each try to help save one addict before it's too late.

Dan Kreuter

Philadelphia 2024

MATT MAN: A LOVE STORY

Rest in Peace Matt Man, my beautiful son; may your words endure and speak from the grave to help those in need.

Karen, Mike, & Matt

EARLY DAYS

- Tuesday
- Philadelphia Love Song
- Big Mike
- A Walk in the Sun

Matt and Cousin Jessie

Tuesday

Matt wrote this on September 12th, 2001, right after 9/11. He
was 12 years old.

Why here/why now Why so close to our town?
Our country/our ground When we hear the news we Dare not say a
sound
When you think about it you can't Find a way to giggle
You could be the toughest Man and even fear
A little

So much happiness all around you Then it crumbles down, right
In front of you

Our country in panic Everyone all twisted up in one hammock
We all have to stop And take a look
Or in 10 years read It in a book
Read about terrible Tuesday – a sad day More sad than
A depressing play.

This day This day Tuesday

Matt loved Philadelphia, but the mean streets of Philadelphia are Ground Zero for addicts and the streets fed his addiction and ultimately killed him. You can find drugs anywhere in America, I know, but take a trip to K&A one day and you'll know what I mean. He composed this poem in High School - was it teenage angst or did it foretell the darkness to come?

Philadelphia Love Song

I am..

Spelling Love within a square The bushes circled in dirt

A clumsy clothespin high City Hall in Baroque

The pigeon on the sidewalk scavenging for scraps

Or maybe the schoolboy reaching for a smoke in his pack The

tourists taking pictures of a dead explorer in cast Perhaps the

mouth of the subway swallowing faces unknown Bustling

businessmen with hearts made of glass

The now dwarfed church casting shadows below A boarded-

up magazine stand with nothing to sell The flags down the

parkway embracing the wind Mostly the traffic bunching up by

the dozens

Or am I the crazed one proclaiming the end?

This is a homage to his big brother whom he loved and admired. He became estranged from Big Mike, but Big Mike never quit on him.

I lost a son. Mike lost his brother. Hard to know what's worse…

Big Mike

"In order to hear Pink Floyd, you have to listen to them."

The words from my brother's mouth still ring in my ears as if he just said them.

It is the late summer of 2001, and my brother and I are sitting in his beige Eddie Bauer edition Ford Explorer, two brothers sharing a moment that, to this day, transcends any lesson I have ever received. Mike was off to college in a week, and although five years apart, we were closer than any other siblings I knew of. On paper, Mike was not the greatest role model. He did not have a 4.0. He made mistakes. He was not perfect. However, if anything is said about my brother it is that he is the most beloved person I have ever known. And for years, I wondered why. At 6'7, two-hundred and eighty pounds, Mike seemed like the type of person who intimidated most people, not one to draw them in. Yet he always had people around him. It seemed as if everywhere we went, someone knew him. "Big Mike!" they would yell. In a way, I suppose, I tried to act as an opposite to my brother. We were and are very close; but it bewildered me that even if he did something wrong, everyone

16

still loved him. It frustrated me. I could not seem to find who I really was. All my life I was tagged as "Big Mike's little brother" and it bothered me. I'm Matt.

I'll admit, I was selfish.

"I'm funnier, I'm better looking, I'm smarter," I told myself.

So why do I not receive the love that Mike garnered? It was not as if I did not have friends. I was popular, but the difference between Mike and I was that although I was popular, he was loved.

Now I know why everyone loves him the way that they do. It did not have to do with his looks, or his physical prowess or anything. It was his selflessness. And it all goes back to that late summer's day in his car. Mike was not talking about music or Pink Floyd at all. He was talking about life. What Mike was illuminating on was the fact that one has to listen to other people, not just hear what they have to say. Mike is beloved because of his ability to listen to people. Being listened to is a very underrated aspect of life and people appreciate it more than they think.

As I go into my senior year, the words that my brother told me six years ago still influence me greatly. I no longer have self-serving friends but friends who love me. And it is not for egotistic reasons, but because I adamantly strive, myself, to listen to my friends. And in a world that is growing more and more deaf, my brother has taught me that a little listening goes a long, long way.

I never knew how much Matt enjoyed our time together playing golf, a sport I am not very good at but one that he was.

It's so sad to read him say *"I know I will love the game when I am 80 years old..."*

When he didn't come close to stacking the sober days and making the turn.

St Andrews, in happier times

A Walk in the Sun

When writing a personal essay on an important relationship in my life, I know I should be writing about a family member, an ex or current girlfriend, perhaps a high- school teacher who inspired me to be great. Well, I am not going to write about any of those things. I am going to write on my love and utter admiration for the game of golf, and the passion, relationships and awe-inspiring moments of glory that comes along with it. For me, golf is the ultimate. The way the grass feels around my cleats, I can almost feel as if I am a part of the course sometimes. Standing there, encompassed by all the elements Mother Nature can produce, the sun slowly fading into the summer sky, it is truly a transcendent feeling. The sight of a tiny, white ball getting launched into that clear, blue sky is more beautiful to me than all of the art in the world. What is most important is the man I have become since taking the game up, and the strong bonds I have formed with not only my father and friends but the lessons I have taken with me along the way.

I started playing when I was twelve, a tall, scrawny product of countless summers of baseball and the fall and winter consumed with basketball. It was my father, a late comer to the game of golf as well (he started playing when he was forty) who first introduced me to the game. I was hooked immediately. I started my career at the chip'n putt at Woody's Driving Range, a collection of raggedy par three holes, but to me it might as well have been Augusta National. As an athlete, I did not think it would take much for me to succeed at this new endeavor. I could not have been more wrong in my life.

20

After a couple of rounds, I was certain that only mad men played such a stupid and frustrating game. But it was in this frustration that my love for the game began to grow.

It did not take me long to become a good golfer. By fifteen I was shooting in the eighties consistently and showed signs of glory along the way. But as I was maturing so did my understanding of what golf was really about. Golf is a gentleman's game. It is the only sport where there are no officials to call fouls. You, the player, are your own official. As a young man I learned almost instantly the qualities of honesty and integrity, and how to exhibit them not only on the golf course, but off it as well. Golf is special to me in a number of ways, but perhaps the most dearest to me is the bond it has strengthened between my father and I. Golf is our thing.

Any given Sunday in the summer you will find my father and I, out there in the wilderness, swinging away in the summer light. I cannot describe to non-golfers what it is like to be with the ones you love out on the course. It is such a surreal feeling of companionship, walking those miles together, sharing shots that end in disaster and sometimes those that end in triumph, that it is honestly hard to describe in words. Golf demands a hundred percent of your attention, and by doing so it is the best therapy in the world. When faced with a two-hundred yard shot over water or a fifteen-foot curving birdie putt, nothing else in the world matters. Golf has the power to make you forget about any troubles in your life and forces you, only if for a couple of hours, to direct all of your focus into playing a perfect round.

Now here I am, a college student with a handicap of zero, and yet I am as enamored with the game as I was when I was twelve. And it is never one specific factor that makes golf the greatest game ever invented. Is it the way the game can turn a no-nonsense business executive into a happy-go- lucky teenager? The respect and courtesy years of the game has taught me? The way my dad and I relax, unwind and spend quality time in each other's company? It is all these things and more that make golf such an important relationship to me. Because I know I will love the game when I am eighty years old, and golf will be right there to love me back.

Golf shows the true identity of a man, through eighteen holes every emotion in the human body surfaces; and it is in those moments when the true nature of a person is revealed. I have been inspired and obsessed by the game ever since I first picked up a club and it is the lessons; I have learned along the way that have made me the person I am today. Golf has given me the confidence to be my own person, the humbleness to know when I am wrong and the integrity to admit my own mistakes. All in all, golf has been one gigantic life-lesson, and I haven't even made the turn yet.

Blues and Despair

Why did an outwardly happy boy with a lust for life have such deep-felt despair?

- No Blues
- Jesus Christ
- Long Live The Blues
- Confetti
- Like Eating Glass
- Toxicity
- Psychodrama Poppy Flower
- Stars and Symbols

No Blues

There are no blues
That can sound quite as heartfelt as mine.
Lamented at the gorge of the river,
I watched them weep their banks dry.
I hum the sorriest tunes On the bars of these dives,
Send all the patrons running home To make up with their first wives.

My prose is purple,
But not as pretty as lucerne. For sweet nothings from the lips of gargoyles
Nobody ever yearned. Perpetually a Philistine
But darling I am longing to learn.
Been looked at like
The rotten grape on the vine
While you and yours are drinking sauternes.

But the low
Is what I came for And to bask
In a darkness I do adore

I am the raven's solo,
The sorrow that makes you salute. Pounding the earth for the early worm
I am a glutton but it's good for my glutes.
I was solace to the sirens,
The bait to the fisherman's rod – the hook took me far from my family,
But closer to God.

24

Jesus Christ

Jesus Christ, that's a pretty face,
The kind you'd find on someone I could save.
And if they don't put me away, Well, it would be a miracle.
Do you believe you're missing out,
That everything good is happening somewhere else?
But, with nobody in your bed The night's hard to get through

And when I die
Do I divide or pull apart? 'Cause my light is too slight To hold back all my dark.

Well, Jesus Christ I'm alone again,
So, what did you do those 3 days you were dead? 'Cause this problems going to last
More than the weekend.
And Jesus Christ I'm not scared to die, I'm a little bit scared of what comes after –
Do I get the gold chariot?
Do I float through the ceiling?

And when I arrive

I won't know anyone And this ship went down In sight of land.
And at the gates
Does Thomas ask to see my hands?

And I know you come in the night like a thief
But I've had some time, oh Lord, to hone my lying technique.
And I know you think that I'm someone you can trust, But I'm scared I'll get scared
And I swear I'll try to nail you back up.
So, do you think that we can work out a sign?
So I know it's you and that it's over So I won't even try.
And I know you'll come for the people like me, We all got wood and nails,
We turn out hate in factories. We all got wood and nails
And we sleep inside of this machine.

Long Live the Blues

I pushed your head down, Flat onto the page.
I held the weapon, Flat against your face.
I remembered the promise
That I had to make - And turned the pen back, Back onto myself.

So, you can stick your words of comfort And you can keep your well
wishes, too.
Singing, "I got the blues," 'Cause they hold me closer Than you
would ever do – Long live the blues.

I know your shape And I know your size,
You are the weight of the concrete boots That pull me under the
tide.
And now you're marching on To a different drum,
Leaving my body here without a beat. A body drained of all feeling

Could be nothing but a piece of meat.
This lump in my throat Is the knot that you tied
With a flick of your tongue And a wink of your eye

I've been sitting sidesaddle in the devil's chair I've been muddying
upholstery, you didn't care
We've been clinking glasses into the dead of night But your fire
keeps me warm and keeps my heart alive

Confetti

Confetti floats away,

Like dead leaves in the wagon's wake. There were parties

here in my honor, 'til you sent me away

And now silver moons belong to you

I'm off to the ballet –

And to practice all these ancient ways. Tell the new kids

where I hid the wine, Tell their fathers that I'm on my way

soon.

And I believe in growing old with grace, I believe she only

loved my face.

How Long?

Tough choice, don't make me laugh. My life's a mess, your life's a gas.
You broke my heart at Midnight Mass, Now I'm the ghost of Christmas past.
The only choice you gave to me, Is one I took reluctantly,
You used to play democracy, Gave me thine eyes so I could see

How long? How long?
How long 'til we sink to the bottom of the sea?
How long 'til it's only you and me?

What's the point in getting clean? You wear the same old dirty jeans. What's the point in being seen?
Those eyes are cruel, those eyes are mean.
What's the point in human beings?
A sharpie face on tangerines – All masked up like Halloween,
Just living in the in-between,
I've seen no one's face behind the scenes, Well, at least not convincingly.

Getting to the top

Wasn't supposed to be this hard – The car is down on Kelly
drive.
My house is up the boulevard.
The registrations here with me, But neither of us has the key.
We should move down to the flats

Like Eating Glass

It's so cold in this house Open mouth swallowing us
The children sent home from school Will not stop crying

And I know that you're busy Do I know that you care?
You got your fingers on the pulse You got your eyes
everywhere And it hurts all the time
When you don't return my calls And you haven't got the time
To remember how it was

It's so cold in this house It's so cold in this… Like drinking
poison Like eating glass

Toxicity

*I'm still haunted by your ghost, It's the thing that scares me
most – Your taste, I fear, has come to stay Spoils all others,
keeps love at bay.*

*It's only you I see in dreams,
Well, looks like you meant more than it seems.
Gotta get you out of my head, Forever fill the space in my bed.*

*You're a demon on the loose, I'm the neck and you're the
noose. I'm just a body that you left to sway.
Underneath my dangling feet you play.*

*It's always you behind the door, It's always me sprawled on
the floor.
Wishing I could change the past, Wishing this heartache
wouldn't last.*

*There was no me without you, This is the first thing I have to
do. Reestablish my sense of self,
Us together is bad for my health*

Psychodrama Poppy Flower

You're my psychodrama poppy flower Moonlight drips in the
magic hour Standing atop Babel tower.
You speak my tongue with such power

Stars and Symbols

You asked if you could see me Before I went away.

You didn't give a reason, Didn't know what you would say.

But I was hoping that the breath from my face Would blow
every last thing into place

The bedspread decked in moons and stars And symbols of the
star signs –

How you read how mine applied To how I would be sex-wise

And in my arms you disappeared And I seemed twice the size

We slept and woke with lips together, Sleeping felt like lies.

Girl I helped you with your demons But your ghosts are now
haunting me, too.

But if we tiptoe through the true bits, We might make it to the
other side

What doesn't kill you leaves you wounded, Will nurse you
better, make it all alright.

Love Poems

"For we are two souls intertwined, and our love will echo throughout all time"

- Scranton girl
- Kind of Girl
- Sunken Stone
- Water and Fire
- Island Girl

Scranton Girl

Matt wrote and recited Scranton Girl at the wedding of his brother Mike and Breanne, who met each other at the University of Scranton

We met in such a cold, dark place.
Which suddenly became much brighter, When I happened across your face.
My heart stopped and everything felt lighter. As I took in your beauty, your aura, your grace.
After that first glance, I knew it was you, so I Followed you across campus, the classrooms and the bars.
To be together there was nothing we wouldn't do.
Because some romances are just written in The stars.
And seeing your smile makes me know that's true.
So, we built a love over the following years.
From dorm rooms and those funky Scranton houses. Through

MATT MAN: A LOVE STORY

laughter and parties and down-days and tears.
Through new places, new jobs, new shoes and new blouses.
And no matter what comes next, as long as I'm with you I'll
Have no fears
Because I am yours and you are mine. And that is why we're
Here today. Nothing in this world is quite as fine. And nothing
Will ever stand in our way. For we are two souls intertwined,
And our love will echo throughout all of time.

Kind of Girl

She's the kind of girl That makes you sell your soul.
She's the kind of girl That takes a serious toll.
She's the kind of girl That makes your nights hazy.
She's the kind of girl That's the best kind of crazy.

I'm haunted by your ghost, It's the thing that scares me most
Your taste, I fear, has come to stay, Ruins all others, keeps new love at bay

You're a demon on the loose.
I'm the neck and you're the noose. I'm the body that you leave to sway. 'Neath my
dangling feet you play.

It's only you I see in dreams, Looks like you mean more than it seems.
Gotta get you out of my head, Forever fill the space in my bed.

There was no me without you, This I know I must now do.
Reestablish my sense of self, Us together is bad for my health
It's always you behind the door, It's always me sprawled on the floor.
Wishing I could change the past, Wish these heartaches wouldn't last.

Cut my heart out on silver plate,
St. Peter gave me the keys to her heavenly gate.
Big bang, worlds collide.
Sleep with lips together, side by side.

She's the kind of girl That ruins all others. She's the kind of girl
That makes you forget your brothers.
She's the kind of girl
That makes you forget yourself.
She's the kind of girl
Makes you feel good with bad health.

Sunken Stone

I'm sinking like a stone in the sea.
I'm burning like a bridge for your body.
I'm sinking like a stone in the sea.
I'm burning all the roads that lead towards me.

I wonder what it is that you see? Your eyes hint at who I could
be. But if seeing really is to believe, I'd wish you shut your
eyes – Grant me reprieve
I'm just scared at who I've become.
You deserve the most, I can only give some.
And maybe one day I'll be that man in your head, But, for now,
I'll lay broken, sunken in bed.

Just know that your beauty shines through, And the fire in my
heart burns ever true.
I wish I could stoke yours, rekindle that flame, Reanimate the
sound of when you call out my name.

Trying to Recover

A pair of Recovery Poems- there was hope here, there was light just for a while.

"My Pen and I" and "Recovery"

My Pen and I

Summer without you is as cold is winter Winter without you is

even colder; I try and remain

resourcefully young

Without you I feel progressively older.

Without you I feel like a darkly deep chasm Widening each

second as my days grow longer; I try to mind

the gap with a number of things

That are as useful as a ship without any harbor.

I know it is trite to write my woes down in rhyme Mourning a

woman I'll never touch again; But I can't seem to

think of a better way to cope

Then to keep you alive you with the stroke of my pen.

So I'll write and I'll write 'til I'm all out of words Write 'til the sun

is shrunken and dry; Living this life without you is onerous

I'll be blissful when at last my pen and I die.

Recovery

We come in here these broken things, Broken down on broken wings -

Dead eye stares. Soul stripped bare.

So frightened of what the future brings.

Replaying regret from our past; Our lives are hopeless, the die is cast.

All out of love, No help from above,

Repeatedly chasing the first til our last.

But there's a way out of despair, to go from drowning to the freshest of air.

Admit defeat, Don't dare retreat.

Because there is a path from here to there.

There is a way back from drugging and drinking if you can find it in you to

change your thinking - And trust me it's hard,

To let go: discard:

The past behaviors that left your sinking.

But I promise you'll find

A slight change in your mind-And fraction by fraction, You'll start to take

action

And begin to leave your old life behind.

And with this new view on living, You'll be amazed what you've given.

Fear and guilt slip away. Inner peace comes to stay -

People actually want what you are now bringing.

Stay open and humble And if you shall stumble - Get up off the ground.

Let the world hear the sound

Of your unstoppable, raucously raging rumble.

Lightning Storm Lightning Storm Redux

- Lightning
- Lightning Storm
- Lightning Storm Redux

Lightning

*Poets see sunrises, sunsets, and even lightning storms in a
whole different way
Lightning Storm is my favorite of all his poems. "…a little
sound goes a long way." When I read it out loud I cry
for all that might have been.*

Lightning Storm

Early one morning,

A lightning storm soaring, Stopped by to show me its play.

It's only just touring, Which could render it boring,

But my god, I could not look away.

The sky was asunder,

As the light danced its number - Beckoning the dawn into day.

But as I stared up in wonder, How I longed for some thunder -

A little sound goes a long way

Lightning Storm Redux

Lightning storm You're my dream And I've been torn
Come outside and calm me down Cause when you strike
My heart is found

Lightning storm Flash your light
And make me warm
Do you want to come over and kill some time?
Keep telling me facts And I'll be fine

Lightning storm Guide me to your home
Through the bushes, through the thorns I'll stay the night
Pass the salt, pour the wine Together we will be alright

LAST DAYS

I'm not sure when Matt wrote this, but the end was surely near.

Heart Cooks Brain

I'm on my way to God, don't know

My brain's the burger and my heart's the coal

I'm trying to get my head clear,

I push things out through my mouth.

I get refilled through my ears.

I'm on my way to God, don't know or don't care.

My brain's the weak heart And my heart's the long stairs.

Inland from Jersey shores, The ravens and the seagulls

Push each other inward and outward.

The Awakening

My eyes have fallen asleep

The bitter world has sewn them shut: Shortly though, I will

wake up,

And arise to the sight of the splendid sun.

Gleaming down and greeting all, Cleansing the hurt off of

everyone.

I'll awaken to a world I see, In the last corner of my mind-

A mental garden, a sprawling green, Ripe with flowers, a tall

Ash tree.

But what I see is all cold, What I see is not right.

All the hope in this world, Gets cemented in fright.

So, for now, I'll stay dreaming,

In fear of awakening too soon - These tear-freezing winds Will

slay me in bloom.

For with no garden, To solicitously tend, While I hazily sleep;

My mind will turn a bitter cold

And be but snowfall to somberly sweep.

My eyes They are asleep.

Be There Soon

In this house, There's no order.
There's no loss of love out here If it's over.

And though I called Out to you;
Something is haunting these four walls, They know it's true.

I will crawl Right back to you
Under the swollen summer sky I'll be there soon

I've been told, told Of the new fast days
There's some room to breathe, But darling don't think twice.
We'll be there soon.

Halcyon Bells

Where were you 10 years ago?
When I was finding out what this meant
Fumbling around in the backs of cars, Sneaking into dark lit
bars,
Now, my youth has long been spent.

Where were you 5 years ago?
When I was too busy getting high. Sleeping out most every
night,
Actively shunning the dreary daylight.
Idling my best gears by.

Where were you a year ago? After my baby said farewell?
We tried to make it last, Too hard rekindling the past,
The distant ringing of halcyon bells.

IOUs

After one or two I get used to the room We go slow when we

first make our moves

By five or six I'll bring you out to the car

By number nine I got my head in the bar And it's sad but true

Out of cash and IOUs.

Water

We sent out the S.O.S. call
It was a quarter past four in the morning When the storm broke our
second anchor line Four months at sea, four months of calm sea
Only to be pounded in the shallows off the hip of Montauk Point.

They call them rogues, they travel fast and alone One-hundred-foot
faces of God's good ocean gone wrong What they call love is a risk,
cause you will always get hit Out of nowhere by some wave and
end up on your own

Your tongue is a rudder That steers the whole ship
Sends your words past your lips
Or keeps them safe behind your teeth. But the wrong words will
strand you Come off course while you sleep
Sweep your boat out to sea or dashed to bits upon the reef.

The vessel groans the ocean's pressure its frame
Off the port I see the lighthouse through the sleet and the rain.
And I wish for one day to give my love and repay debts

But the morning finds our bodies washed up thirty miles west.
They say that the captain stays fast with the ship Through still and
storm
But this ain't the Dakota, and the water is cold

Water & Fire

The water starts to rise, You're trying hard to breathe, You're
burning up inside
It's getting hard to see.
There's nowhere else to hide,
There's nowhere else to be –So turn within the hide Until you
turn to me.

Wipe the salt from your eyes, But leave it on your skin.
So when I taste your thighs
I know exactly where you've been. And if our bond should
sever ties,
Sometime after we begin, After all of our goodbyes I'll still
taste you deep within.

But if this is meant to last, A spark that turns to fire,
Then I have so much love to cast – And that love will never
tire.
So take my hand to grasp As we climb forever higher,
Keeping pain within the past And our future will transpire.

MATT MAN: A LOVE STORY

Matt loved The Great Gatsby and all things F Scott Fitzgerald. This quote was circulated by a business associate of mine and seems fitting, and hopeful.

For what it's worth:
It's never too late or, in my case, too early to be whoever you want to be. There's no time limit, stop whenever you want. You can change or stay the same, there are no rules to this thing. We can make the best or the worst of it. I hope you make the best of it. And I hope you see things that startle you.
I hope you feel things you've never felt before. I hope you meet people with a different point of view. I hope you live a life you're proud of. If you find that you're not, I hope you have the strength to start all over again.

F. Scott Fitzgerald

Made in the USA
Middletown, DE
12 September 2024